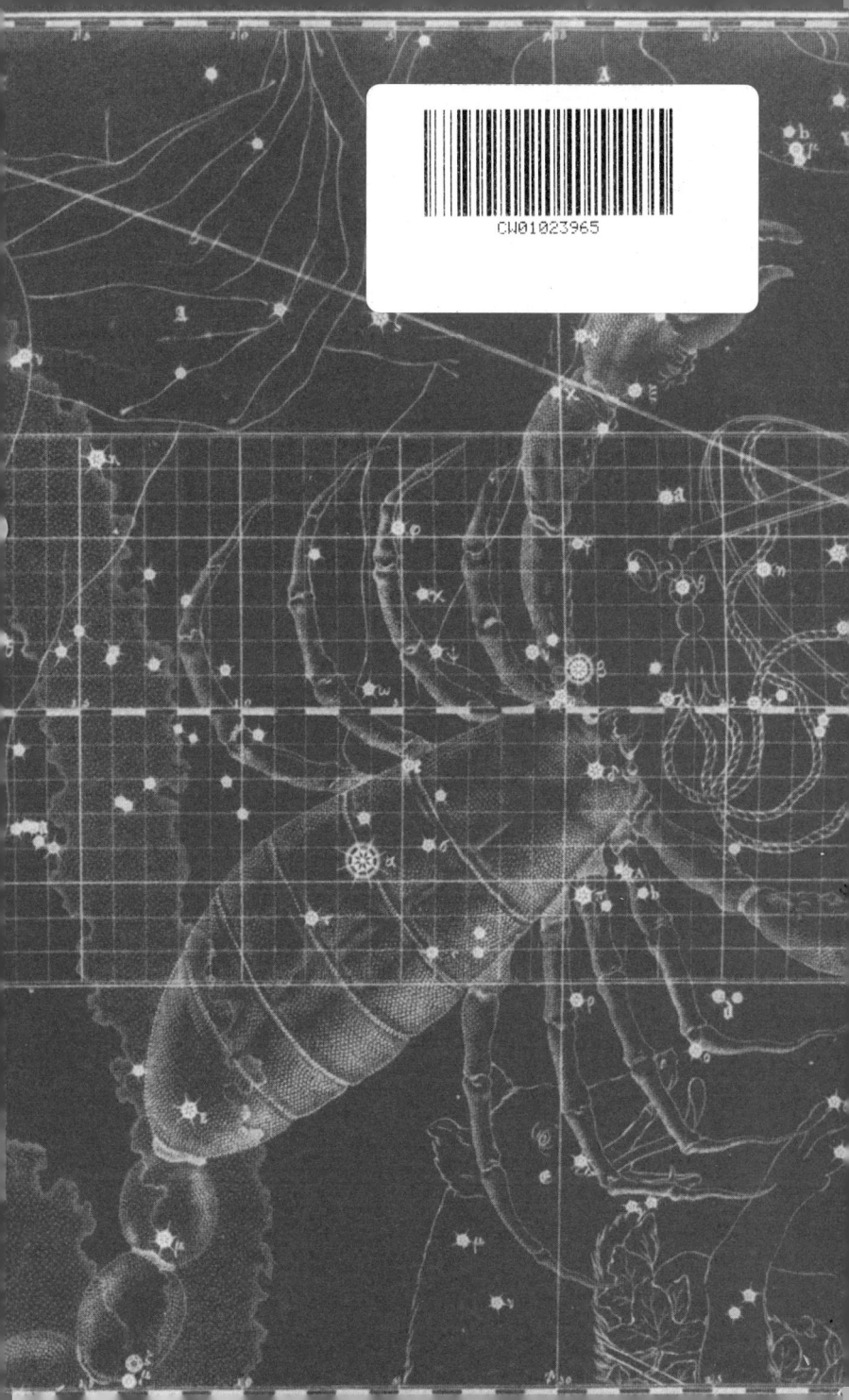

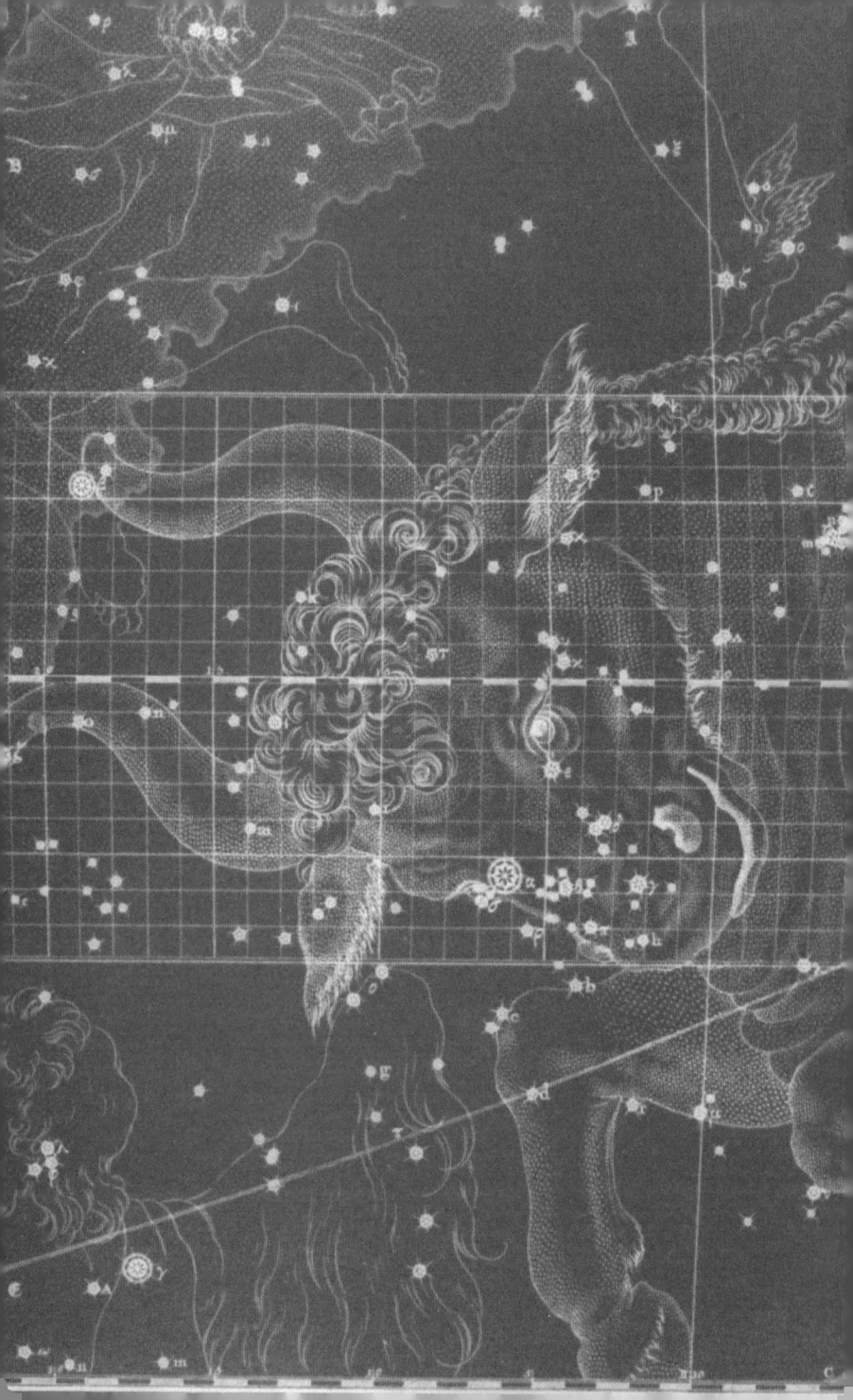

SWIM

*poems
by*

Pat Borthwick

First published 2005
by

Mudfog Press
c/o Arts Development
The Stables
Stewart Park
The Grove
Marton
Middlesbrough
TS7 8AR

www.mudfog.co.uk

Copyright © Pat Borthwick 2005
All rights reserved

Cover Design, Layout and Print by James Cianciaruso
based on ideas and suggestions from the author
Copyright © 2005

Images on cover and endpapers courtesy of Atlas Celeste
by John Beris c1750, with thanks to Michael Oates
of the Manchester Astronomical Society.

ISBN 1-899503-63-3

Mudfog Press is a member of
The Independent Northern Publishers
www.northernpublishers.co.uk

Mudfog gratefully acknowledges
the support of
Arts Council England
and Middlesbrough Council

SWIM

Previous publications:

Between Clouds and Caves
Littlewood Arc 1988

Pamphlet collections:

Deep Waters
Pharos Press 1996

Monkey Puzzles
Pharos Press 1996

Zig-Zags
Pharos Press 1998

Hospital Corners
Pharos Press 2000

Being Alive
Bloodaxe 2004

Other books by the same author:

Chalk Marks – The Wolds' Longest Poem
(A Year of the Artist Publication 2002)

upshoots
Howardian Hills AONB 2003

Sheds
2004

On CD:

*Real*Estate *(allotment sheds and their owners)* 2001
Chalk Marks 2002
upshoots 2003

for Galileo, Moose & Lubadsagush

Contents

10   Staring at Stars

11   Moon Landing While Magritte Searches for Something to Put in His Pipe

13   Patrick Moore Blows a Fuse

14   Deer

15   At The Observatory

17   Flat Earth

18   Bought Cakes *(sequence)*

22   Bidding

24   Kleptomaniac

26   Power-Cut Candles

28   Forest

29   Out of Bounds

30   Mum's The Word

32   Piano

34   Swim *(sequence)*

41   On the Underground

42   Nocturne

43   Snake

45	Murder
47	Where We Once Lived
48	Hospital Corners *(sequence)*
58	Hedge
60	Seeds
61	Leaves
62	Learning About Bats
64	Draft
66	Letters *(sequence)*
69	Late Road Home
70	Charcoal Burner
71	Unicorn
72	Tables
73	Clear Night

Acknowledgements are due to the following publications:

Aesthetica, The Aesthetica, Algol (The Astronomical Society Magazine), Dream Catcher, Dress of Nettles, Hospital Posters N.E., The Interpreter's House, Lancaster Lit Fest anthologies, Making Worlds (Headland), Mslexia, Poetry in the Parks (Sigma Press), Poetry Life, Poetry Monthly, Poetry Nottingham, Sheffield Thursday, The Poetry Cure (Bloodaxe Books), Writers' Forum, Yorkshire Journal.

Poems in this collection have been competition prize-winners in:

The Barnet Open, The Bedford Open, Blue Nose Poets, Chester Open, East Street Poets, Hastings, Hospital Arts N.E., Ilkley Lit Fest, LACE, Lancaster Lit Fest, Leicester Open, Newark, Nottingham, Manchester Open, Moor and More, Myeloma Awareness, The Petra Kenney, Poets Anonymous, Poetry Life, Ragged Raven, Second Light, Sheffield Thursday, Ware Poets Open.

The author wishes to thank the Hawthornden Foundation and the staff at the castle for providing her with the quiet opportunity and ambience in which to complete 'Swim'.

Staring at Stars

'We enquire of the spinning stars how we began,
but our question merely glances off them
and returns to us unanswered.'

Jean Orizot

Grandmothers, Great Grandmothers, is that you
spinning open-armed beyond the astrolabe
and armillary? Old telescopes? Apollo?
You are far away in tired light, and already further,
zipping through the pages of my almanac with Tippex.
Now how can I tell the hour to plant the wheat,
which wood to cut, when to serve warm figs
for Jed to overspoon with cream?

Jed and I have drunk the last of your parsnip wine.
Our goblets are upturned. We've got cream everywhere.
Hoof to hoof, horn to horn, starry breath to hay breath,
celestial beasts above our barn embrace our own.
Ploughs turn curvatures of nocturnal tilth all leading back
to you Grandmothers, Great Grandmothers. Ad infinitum.
They say that to be far away means to return
so we'll soon be there to meet you coming back.

Taurus: ring now for an in-depth forecast to your advantage.
Virgo: you must understand that timing is crucial.

On the flipchart in the hundred and five star hotel
Plato describes the harmony of the world.
He draws a ladder and a mundane egg, some spirals.
And when Hubble says *space is constantly expanding*
they grip their chairs. Tighter still when he continues,
we are moving away from ourselves at great speed.
Someone dares to ask what on earth would happen
if something like another meteorite crashed down.

Don't worry, he says. *We'll be going over it again. If there's time.*

Moon Landing While Magritte Searches for Something to Put in His Pipe

Carefully, prise off the Arctic cap. Set it to one side.
Mind it doesn't slide away. Find chisels, a shark-head hammer
and, starting from the centre, walk round, chipping at the plateau ice
until you've hollowed out a bowl big enough to hold the moon.
Mind your eyes - ice-chits of aquamarine, turquoise, cerulean blue
will fly up then tinkle down in rhomboids, parallelograms,
diamonds. There's bound to be a walrus tusk, whalebones
or maybe some corrugated tin the last lot left.

Use these to tidy up. Or cod-head scoops.

Stars begin to pinball,
dance their constellations high above the ice.
They peer down into the cavern of a proffered bowl.

The moon floats up
opening its fullness like a flower.

It sees the cap has shifted.
It sees the crater in the ice.
It sees a man.

His thoughts of thermo-gloves, and hollowing out a bowl
trawl through space with Mozart, Desert Island Discs,
spent canisters, text messages, a dead monkey.

The man is holding a long-handled rake.
He reaches up into the night until its head
is lodged behind the moon's circumference.
As though winding in a silver kite,
he draws it down into the hole.

A perfect fit.
An eye's orb in its socket, a mouse-ball in a laptop.
Now a pale moonface, framed in ice, stares out at stars,
its open mouth amazed at parallax, perspective,
how familiar points have vanished.
Drag the ice-cap over. Moonlid.

What happens next is faster than a blink.
Cod-boats can't plot a course, are slipping back.
Gulls fall silent, wheel out in one thick airborne raft
towards a curvature they'll never reach.
Down below in Spitzbergen and Storgenfjord
the automatic genny lights are flashing on.
Midnight. The Arctic Circle is a blaze of electricity
and all the spaceships out there are informed *we have a problem*.
In the non-light of night *to consider the options carefully.* Fast.

Patrick Moore Blows a Fuse

All day, way off the Beaufort scale,
the winds have taken vent.
The whole Earth rocks in their wake.
Weather cocks, wind socks, cones
skylark miles above our chimneys.
This island seems swept out to sea,
a Roaring Forties
wrenching out whole forests
turning gutters into rivers,
the rivers into rush hour waves.
And us, blown or bobbing somewhere.
Of course, the lines are down.

In his domed and rattly house
Patrick Moore, with a wobbling candle,
searches through his cupboards.
He finds boxes of charged particles,
old tins of quarks. His drawers are filled
with faded nebulae and quasars, dead stars.
On the bowed steel shelves, white dwarves.
Everywhere there's dust. Cosmic dust.
It claims the position of things.
Look, beneath Galileo's bust and these books,
a layer of varnished newness, then under here,
the circular base shape of this astrolabe.

He shuffles in his Glo-Moon slippers.
Nowadays spiral stairs are difficult to climb
although climb he must, to press his eye
against the eyepiece and see neon blues
arc between the fingertips of galaxies,
to watch winds at 1,000 mph scour planets,
to scan for a future comet with his name.
But first to find a screwdriver and fuse,
to mend the plug, its copper wires
frayed and fanned like solar flares.
He's eager for more light years
that might illuminate a vanishing today.

Deer

Caught in the sweep of my headlights,
from over the dark queue of hawthorn,
a deer pedals upwards in air
until stars ride her back
and her eye is all moon.
Why she was called from her cover
is only known to herself and the night.

Night Princess in your glittery gown,
please allow me the time, as you
float and freewheel, to open an ash-leaf fan
and pretend to avert my gaze
then chase after sounds
that escape from my throat and into the car
while you are the silence of amber and moss.
Then gone.
Reabsorbed.
Among antlers and gloss.
Lost between shadows of trees.
You moved in language I shouldn't have seen,
a script of pale symbols flitting through bushes
then airborne with code secreted in fur.

I know that flowers throw away
only their unwanted perfume,
so the truth has to be
that the glimpse you allowed me
was what you'd already discarded,
did not choose to keep.

At The Observatory

For Martin

I'm waiting for my turn to climb the spiral
staircase to the six inch refractor
trained within a fraction of an eyelash

on the rim of a planet a billion miles away.
I'm eager to reach the polished eyepiece,
to adjust the knurled brass focus wheel.

A man is talking chemistry and numbers
with necklaces of noughts. He's talking
dust and snowball rings, shepherd-moons.

But it's all above my head until suddenly
I'm looking through the scope and
Saturn's mine, tilted like that cup and saucer

spinning from your hand the day I said
it'd take more than milky statues or a saint's
scrawny toe to have me still believe in God.

You've worn out rosaries for me since,
lit candles everywhere. But how can I
when, with each turn of my spade, soil bleats?

While smoke bleeds from every blade of grass?
And when, a few gates down the road,
Orion strides across our hollow barn? It's

lambing time. The family should be playing
astral dot-to-dot with one eye on the ewes.
The Saturn man tunes the lens to Titan.

Beyond the pock-marked moon's ecliptic path
the night fold is the same dark, only deeper.
Stone huts flicker in the fields, as we do,

as the white stars do in theirs, before
being rounded up then spindled one by one
into an impenetrable and far unknown.

Flat Earth

So what does it matter
if we still believe the world is flat?
How can it not be? Each October,
after the family plough is honed,
it furrows beside the hawthorn hedge,
waking the fields with silver lines
 straight home to the kitchen table.
We sit around its steaming square,
Bess wagging at all four corners.

Grandparents and great grandparents
watch us from gilt frames.
Their footprints pattern this red soil
treading every hectare, every level acre.
They broadcast flighty seed
from fiddle-drills, then bent to tamp,
to weed, to reach down in the ground
where a chain of hand-bones spanned
through bronze and flint and stone.

Still does. Surely if the world were round
then at those times when one of us
sensed something beyond the five-bar,
after packing and setting off, eventually
they'd arrive back from the opposite horizon,
the farm ahead growing with each stride.
But every year now a few must trip or stumble,
perhaps on a cornerstone, slip or free-fall
over an unfenced boundary edge.

Bought Cakes

I

Staring us in the face it was. What
else, with the wagons on the verge
refusing to come up our drive?
March was different,
coming for the ewes.
We were all green then.
Some in lamb
and all them little wet-lambs.
Can't fault the men. I
stayed in the house with Jen,
managed to pull a curtain off its track.
First row we'd had in thirty years
and some game show on the telly,
two families, all teeth
and clapping when they lost.

II

That night in bed,
between long case chimes,
Jen thought she heard a bleat
coming from the orchard.
Looking down we made out
one they must have missed,
a hungry half-day ghost running
round and round the damsons.
I had to dig it deep,
and the flint I used to tap it.
Our bed seemed smaller after that.

III

And then again, two months on,
the feed bins almost empty
and us ready for new Point of Lays.
Despite all our careful phone calls
the transport refused driving through the gates
to take the old girls. Government instructions.
But no one thought to mention them to us.
We'd two thousand would flow into the field
when Sally barked to wake the cock
and Jen rolled up their metal doors.
Like a tidal wave, all combs and clucks
and feathers and Sally somewhere in there.
You could set the clock by it. Then breakfast.

IV

So, as I said, staring me in the face it was. What else?
I'd have to neck them each by hand, starting after dark.
Jason, just back from university, said I spoke too
soft to hear, and was his boiler suit still hung
behind the door? Eleven-hour shifts we worked,
with one hour off, not stopping till three days on
we saw it done. Our hands were raw, our wrists
and arms and backs in a rhythm that let in pain
once it slowed. Jen had to hold the mug to my mouth,
cut up my food, undo my fly and that.

V

Not too long before the stench wormed
from the shed and under all our doors.
Jace on the tractor, Sally on the trailer with him,
Jen fetching empty paper sacks and rags, me wood,
then down for that drum of sump behind the bales
to cart up to top field. Toppers Feld. Slow.
First time in the lamb barn since.

VI

One match.

VII

Two days before we saw the sky empty of feather ash.
Before that circle cooled. And Sally still not back.

VIII

Jace and I, we don't know what to do.
She's hidden it in the filing cabinet bottom drawer.
Memento Mori. Must be Sal's. It's in an ice-cream box.
Just fits, nose to back of skull. She found it
raking through before we got the digger in.
Won't bury it, like she has her tongue. Gone mute,
won't even wind the clocks or put the kettle on.

IX

Jason's back there and sitting finals now.
The television spills across our knees.
The choice is war, or games
where people wave and laugh a lot.
I read they've unearthed tortoise shells
carved with what might be words,
or attempts at words, from 8,000 years ago,
and that today, three-quarters questioned
didn't know the time it took to soft-boil eggs.
That curtain still needs fixing.
We're managing just fine. Getting by.

X

Will that do? Never did like cameras.
Can you turn it off now? An arts programme?
I'm sorry they were only bought cakes.

In February 2001 Britain's farming communities experienced a devastating outbreak of Foot and Mouth Disease for which the government was unprepared, wrongly advised and, at best, confused. Many farmers had their entire stock slaughtered and never returned to the work their families had known and loved over several generations. The repercussions affected many other lives and livelihoods the length and breadth of the land.

Bidding
Farm auction, Devon 2002

I watch them arrive early,
their little trailers chinkling with lidded churns,
leather harness, long-handled implements.
Down that row on the left, Bert says, reaching
down to slap the numbers on. Wilf and William,
Harry, Len. Their lives are tagged in black and white.
Today, two fifty through to seven ten.

I dream of an usher's cotton gloves,
of gauze and lint and lambswool.
I trawl the cowless corners of their barns.
What more can I do when my heart
fills stone-flagged kitchen drawers,
and, louder than my gavel,
hears the five-bar's ironwork click home?

Through my restless office skylight,
when the bidding's done and they've all gone
to where they still call home, I watch stars
reassemble. Orion has dropped his sword,
ignores hares chasing at his feet. Great Plough
is towed away, no longer works nocturnal land
but hangs from plastic hooks behind the moon.

Tomorrow, in The Paddocks and Field Close,
there'll be trips to fetch fuchsia and geranium.
Their vibrant splash will brighten tops of churns.
The new publican will boast about his bargains
then make rustic features of long-handled tools.
He'll offer free halves to those who come closest
to naming his buys and guess what they used to do.

Change, always change. And who can say for sure
that the future, or today, is less than past? Or more?
Whether at our close we're tagged and set aside
or nourish other crops in astral fields? But as we wait,
like Wilf and William, those four men, our farms
shrink back and rust. Children draw animals in dust.
Wives mop phantom milk from dairy floors.

Kleptomaniac

The Yorkshire coastline from Boulby Cliffs in the north through to Long Nab in the south is collapsing into the sea. It is the fastest disappearing coastline in Europe. The Jurassic sandstone, shale and glacial boulder clay are easy prey for fierce equinoctial tides.

The sea has set its stalls
halfway along the beach.
We rummage through its bric-a-brac,
collect smoothed glass, driftwood,
unusual rusty shapes.

Snatched down from someone's roof,
sucked cornerless,
a marled and sooty stack
sunk into the sand.
Who would have thought to find this here,
brick-red symbol of the heart of home?
And close by,
a whole corner of a house
claimed and prised away
as frightened fingers lost their grip.

Were they prepared,
the family on the sofa by the fire?
It was a familiar sound,
the hungry sea opening wide its jaws,
calling down on the tongue of the wind
into the room. Tweaking the lights.

Generations had heard it so.
Slept with it. When angry,
bellowed at each other over the top of it,
were drowned out and laughed.
The storms come closer, they said.
Kept saying.
Only the gardens shivered and shrunk.

Imagine that sea,
gnashing and grinding and hissing.
A greedy cobble-filled mouth,
world traveller in league with the wind,
defining and looting the land.

Then that house, a home,
raked down on a whim,
to end gobbed at the clay cliff's back
with spittle and trash from the sea.

A kleptomaniac is stamping down this coast.
I WANT! I WANT!

Power-Cut Candles

In dozens or singly
all the corner shops sold candles then.
They nudged each other close in the box,
rattled softly, as I hop-scotched home.
There, in the kitchen,
by the clothes-horse and the stove
I would slide each one out
and place them side by side,
like a waxy raft, on the tabletop.
My palm rolled them this way, that.
The pleasure of that unison,
their yieldiness, their virgin white.

Sometimes, not often, she let me use
the mother-of-pearl penknife
from the second drawer and with the smallest blade
taper one end to fit the holders.
The shavings curled as fragile as our silence,
their crimpled edges
caught the stove's blood-red glow. Quickly
the pile seemed to grow in volume
greater than the candles. I was blissful,
unaware how being older
would melt such mysteries.

On nights when I feared the moon would be
blown from the sky, the power-lines came down.
They fizzed and phuttered the radio,
flickered the lights. Nimble then,
she would fetch the matches and the candles
just before the house switched off.
Only the firelight chattered on the walls

while the wind yawled underneath the curtains,
through every gap. I kept near to myself,
waited for the sanctity of candlelight
knowing it would soften her every feature,
give us reason to draw a little closer.

Forest
For my father

Yes, you must have had the camera
with its cracked leather strap
and celluloid red disc
but I will remember you
by the fullest moon
over the lowest tide on Sutton Sands.

Just the two of us.
Our thirtyish years between
far out at sea that night.
I was seven, seventeen and seventy.
You said to wait and watch,
to listen for that last wave's slap
before the turn. *Sh. Soon!*

Meanwhile, the moon enjoyed the beach.
Scampering, it left silver prints
among the cockleshells
along its flat length.
Soon!

And you stood rock-still,
your eyes constant on the drawn-back
sea. Waiting. Only your gabardine flapped,
sound-tracked the mystery.
Then I knew I didn't want *soon* to begin.
I didn't want our waiting to stop.

Glittering black stumps
emerge from their underwater clay-beds.
Rank after stoic rank horizon.
Fossils glisten in their fissures.
All history now.

Out of Bounds

Their out of bounds bedroom
was a grotto where the low sun
squinnied through the nets
and frisked along the dressing table top
sequinning little jars and bottles.

I would tiptoe in
past the shadow of the bed-end,
to the three silver shark-infested pools,
reflected from the mirrors
deep into the pink shag-pile.

Then, Amami wave set, moisture cream, Vaseline,
each screwtop gasping off, leaving me
to trawl inside. Dab on their secrets.
London Rouge, Evening in Paris, a swansdown puff,
glossy lipsticks you could slide up and down
inside their golden ferrules
fitting the caps over my finger-ends
until my fingers swelled
and pulling those caps off
held the sound of a sudden indrawn breath.
A grenade beyond the gate.

But it was the enamelled peacock compact
with its hidden spring release
I prized the most,
examining its fluorescent blues and greens,
each feather's silky eye
and, inside the lid, freckled with powder,
my own unblinking eye
enlarging and enlarging
as I brought the mirror closer,
this third eye, isolate,
staring over my shoulder at the open door.

Mum's The Word

My cockatoo Cockney aunt, her lips
thirty shades redder than Mother's,
is always flicking back the mirrored lid
of her Parthenon pressed powder compact,
retouching them. She has surprised us again,
arrived with her cases at our front porch.

Auntie Shouty talks and talks and taught me
how to pop the knuckled shells of peanuts
with my thumb, then hold them up
letting the red nuts run down on my tongue.
Vulgar, my mother used to say.
Who's a naughty boy then? she would reply.

Auntie Shouty often shouts or squawks.
She's a Londoner, my mother explains
to the other people on the bus
when they look around,
and see her perched there on the side seat.
At her compact again.
I know her hands are stiffening.
I have to pop the nuts for her, fasten
the feathers on her hat, pin her glitter brooch.

I think my aunt worries that one day
her hands will not lift me
or play music from the fat book she brings,
its notes, blackening the page
like a swirl of pigeons in Trafalgar Square.
She's shown me a photograph of that.
And of someone else with a pigeon on his hat.

She told me this, but *never* to tell my mother,
that every night, before she switches off her light
at (I think) 472, Floor 9, Golders Green, London,
she parts her bedroom curtains as if opening a cage,
follows the star-filled snaking Thames
towards a country called Greece
where *a man in oil* she said she knew once
said he came from. She said my brown eyes
came from there as well.

Piano

Every Christmas the family gathered round it.
The youngest, guided by the oldest hand,
struck a Bluebell match then wobbled it across
to try and light last year's candle stumps.
We always cheered, someone switched the lights off
and after that, curves and lines re-entered
as each shelf and surface of the room
filled with piano, song,
the lark's breath of pages being turned.

Unplanned, the annual programme never changed.
We flickered into moments that were happening.
Our bond strengthened with familiar mistakes
like not remembering every word
and still not sellotaping in page 46. We always ended
with a shanty in memory of Grandad R.N.
who couldn't swim and was lost at sea.
And this is what we understood as family.
Our family.

They say that when Ludwig died
God strengthened the tops of his clouds tenfold
for fear the concert grand came crashing down
in feathery arpeggios and wide white chords. When
Grandma died her clock chimes and our singing
stopped. No one had space for the upright.
It was cleft and chopped, shrunk to five sacks,
its heartstrings plucked and tapped with teaspoons
before the Council carted them away.

But her December notes still play.
They light candles that illuminate the past
and show us things we did not know
then rearrange old thoughts inside our heads
as though moving furniture about a room.
They can surprise you in her sewing box
spooled in tunes you've heard a hundred times
and better for each hearing. Effecting all the family
to hum and tap their feet. Some dead to dance.

Swim

I Dive

Remembering where
could go on forever
with still no certain answers
nor use, but alone,
my sappy back
moulded to warm grass,
ideally a breeze,
I'd let my mind stretch out
through pine-tipped gaps
into the blue.
I'd follow in a perfect dive,
hardly a ripple to disturb
the wisdom of the sky.

Surfacing in this exquisite place
I'd front-crawl towards a cloud
and clamber out
knowing I'd travelled further
than I'd ever been before.
Or anyone. And that from here
I'd understand the Earth,
the Universe, why my parents
had been given to me. Why
it was I wasn't blessed
with Jen's instead.
And how only I had realised
heaven was a mirrored dome
reflecting all the waters
wrapped around the world

including estuaries and oceans,
gravel pits and rivers, reservoirs,
dykes and ditches, lakes, ponds,
puddles and pools and even
goldfish bowls. Even ones with
a dead fish in. Even if I'd killed it
so no-one could take it from me.
And what happened when I sang?
Did my fading notes go somewhere?
Did they wind forever round the stars
to weave a glittering cat's cradle? And
who would I tell all these things to?
And could that be a star fish
nibbling my toe?

II Nets

Seaside shops
and, behind the spinning postcards,
long bamboo canes with gaudy nets.
Rockpools contain the sky
I used to enter. Smaller now,
patinate with wheeling gulls,
they float and wink, while
sandy footprints patter round
before heading off
along each compass point.

I trawl their depth,
scoop ribbon-weed and snails,
a mermaid's purse, a plastic spoon.
But there's a slung weight in my net
that moves, that moves again. That blinks.
That meets my eye darkly. Is fish. Is mine.

III Cast

It's hard to imagine now
who it was spoke first, the blond boy
from the yellow catamaran or me.

But it was he who, standing so close behind
that not even a reed could come between us
and I could feel through his shirt, my blouse,

his morning heat nourish my spine,
with his hands guiding mine, taught me how
to align ferrules, set a rod, tie and bait

my hook, hoop the paternoster, cast,
to tilt a float or let it run downstream, and,
by feathering fingertips along it,

hold tension on the line. And wait.
Perhaps we never spoke.
It's hard to remember now.

But it's harder to forget that first judder,
that first snatch, line spinning from the reel,
that cloudy smell of fish on our fingers.

IV How to use a Renshaw's Hook-Save Disgorger

1.   Hold fish firmly in damp cloth
               (for fish weighing over 13lbs you may need two people).

2.   Draw tension on line.

3. Slide disgorger down along line through the slit and hole on flange to approximately 3 inches from fish's mouth.

4. Tighten line still further.

5. Keep sliding the disgorger down through mouth and into throat.

6. Locate shank of hook. (You will feel disgorger bite on metal.)

7. Make sure you are gripping fish. It may wriggle strongly at this point.

8. Free hook with a wrist-flick i.e. push disgorger down and twist then pull.

9. Repeat until hook is free trying to damage the gullet as little as possible.
   (Remember that only live fish count at weigh-in.)

10. Place fish in keep-net. It may well survive to win you the Match Trophy.

Don't forget to keep your Renshaw's Hook-Save Disgorger handy! Good Luck.

V *Glass Tanks*

Glass tanks line the cobbled streets
fed with hoses spilling polished gems
to rival vaults in Amsterdam. At night,
by tables avalanched with lobster, oyster, prawn,
the 'Carpes Fraiche' tanks glow luminescent.
O-O-O, each pearl of air spins like a rising moon.

That one, she says, pointing her champagne hand.
Later, he sees her slim spine flex
while her dark energy ripples between his sheets.

VI Swam

Fire and ice. Fish have long memories of night.
They swam through stars and planets
strung with bubbling gas like Christmas lights.
They watched us haul ourselves from mud, then,
through our own reflections, stand two-legged,
gill-less, looking down on them. We come
to gawp at them in our sluggish ponds, admire
their bronze amulets and necklaces, their swivel
eyes, their opalescent mouths big enough
to swallow sun, sky, day. We've teetered
on the world's rim for only the time
it has taken them to waft one soft fin.

VII Mud Bubbles

Daily I watch them swim past me.
I see the ripple of their coming,
the mud-bubbles of their lives, surface.
They know I'm here, listening.
They angle for my attention in concentric swirls

then tweak my line, tilt my goose-quill float
against the flow. It dips, it dips again,
runs back across the current
before disappearing down
into the inky slime and reed roots.

I could reel them in, tighten myself
against their shuddering tug,
keep tension thrummed on the line
until they had no place else to be
except drawn into my net.

But today, I let them go, all of them.
Leave them where they are, bottom feeders
gathering the dark into their gills,
filling their deep parchment-coloured bellies
with simple cells. Being there. Knowing

the slow epicure of flavour as it percolates through mud…

VIII Lakeside Lodge

Lakeside Lodge. Gran moves slowly now.
She waits by the aquarium in the foyer
for the chinkle of the trolley. Feeding time.
In each hand, a spread silk fan lifts and falls.
Reflected in lit glass, her solitaire diamond
repeats its tired arc. It sparkles above
mock coral and pagodas, newly hatched carp.

Tonight, she'll watch a comet cross the sky
then swim from the snowy breakers of her bed
to follow on its tail, among butterflies and camels,
chameleons and dodos, scorpions, sheep and snails,
sea goats and dolphins, whales and crabs and hares,
hunting dogs, little lions and lynx, humming birds
winged horses, dinosaurs and dragons, silkworms,
wasps and swans and unicorns and bulls and rams,
sea serpents, crows, amoebae and zebras and,
in this five billion year old star stream,

water boatmen, fish. And kittens. Bears.
They will trail an argent path
as they swim through wheeling galaxies and
perhaps, in one deafening fireball-pulse,
their combined wisdom
will accrete and coalesce
to spin and shape
a new planet's
vestal
heart.

On The Underground

From the moment you buy the ticket
you become a cog engaged in overdrive.
Round curved and tiled corridors,
down escalators plummeting like Niagara Falls,
past ziggurats of posters –
someone strumming their life out –
the machine intakes your breath,
compresses you,
then spits you out on to a platform
where a cool push of air
arrives before the tube train.

MIND THE GAP

MIND THE GAP

MIND THE GAP

but we each stride across it,
looking for all the world
as if we know where we are going,
where we have come from.

Nocturne

Wolf-shadow in the moonlight.
His fingers snapped around our bedroom walls.
My rabbit followed, tried to hold wolf in her paws
but its jaws scissored up the curtains
and the game did not stop there.

Each night the moon travels light,
paddling across rivers, dykes,
shoots waterfalls in a silver canoe.
It strides over mountains, creeps into fields,
drapes along branches to plunder nests.

Hiss of gas, swish of starch,
the midwife slapped you
from a silent pearly blue. Twig-like you dangled
while the harvest moon leant across
to thread you with twisted ribbons.

Blank child, my skyling,
science cannot name
how the moon's circumference
must have balanced on your mood, then
slipped into your blood. Is part of you.

Poor moon, you cry, *can he still see?*
And I reply, *An eclipse, a shadow, it will pass,*
as pressed against cold glass
we watch his one-eyed, yashmaked face
bob darkly.

A door unlatched. Another long night slips in.
It has passed a man with his cases in the street.
Upstairs, you will not sleep. You saw
a wolf at the window, heard his claws on the stair.
Let's talk to the man in the moon, I say.

Snake

Just a glimpse of my bare heel or toe,
the slightest movement of my sheet,
would alert a knotted writhe of snakes
lurking in the cave beneath my bed.
Heavy with poison,
they'd be slung between the springs,
coiled around the metal frame
or simply thick in number, camouflaged
among the carpet pattern's twists and turns,
their bifurcated tongues
wavering between needle-teeth and fangs.
They'd strike at the sight of a pale insole
or ankle, better still, a plumper calf.
When my night screams
brought the man married to my mother
he'd cover my mouth
then reticulate his other hand
between my grooves and hollows.
His tongue, strung with saliva,
would engulf and swallow me
as he delivered his shot of venom.

After the ringing in my ears had stopped
I'd fly into a treetop nest and sway there.
Coach whip, copper head, bull snake,
python, diamond back, smooth snake,
cobra, mamba, sidewinder, hoop snake,
house snake, ophidia, serpentes, my mantra.

I've gained their confidence. *Come up*,
I'll say, and then, in their jewelled tuxedos,
watch them stretch across my pillows,
slither below my duvet. Each time

I am surprised how warm they are,
how sleek their polished scales.
Who'd have guessed I'd have them
eating from my hand? I can
even stroke and squeeze them
while they nudge for more, their dewy eye
not fooling me. I've spent years
learning to unhook my jaw, perfect
the toxicity of my digestive juices
so not a single drop's superfluous.
See how much breath I hold
in this single, elongated lung.
See how I've sloughed my childskin.

Murder

Late on my seventh birthday
my brother murdered somebody
and was asking me, in my pyjamas,
to share and keep his deadly secret.

That night we sat on hessian sacks
in our shadowy allotment shed.
Moonlight slid its tongue
across fork tines and spade shanks.

Upturned terracotta pots
towered on the prick-out bench.
Oil cans occasionally gave off
a metal burp scattering the crawlies.

Still sticky with warm blood
his hands reach for mine,
press something hush-hush
and squelchy-squishy in them.

Eye sockets, he says. *Don't look.*
Let your fingers feel inside.
Eyeballs, he says, swapping them
for something squeezable, moist

but twice as cold. *Teeth. The tongue.*
Piece by piece I hold his slimy crime
and promise a sister's silence.
Then a dumb stump of head.

I know its dome of veinwork, chin,
its wrinkles, cheekbones, twisted nerves.
I know it is our father's. And I know why.
Until the plank door bangs open and

on the jamb hangs his beery profile.
His torch prances across a slatted box
stacked with cut tomatoes, Brussels sprouts,
ten peeled carrots, two kiwis, one courgette,

my brother's hands sparkling with ketchup.

Where We Once Lived

They have ripped down that house,
ground it to dust,
carted its brickwork away.
Now the sun's tongue
probes a new gap
where a wheat field
is seen from the road.

Wheat taller than you,
except from upstairs windows,
where I watched you,
unwind your trails like snails.
The ripening field, warm as a womb.

Then the notice
to pack up our rooms into bags,
pull up the carpets,
pile up a van with our beds,
your toys.

Uproot.

The wheat field,
stiffening,
pricked its ears,
laid low.

We hollowed that house,
the cutlery voicing our anguish.
Milkbottles, homeless,
stared in through the door.

You crayoned your names on the wall.
I filled my apron pocket with husks.
Cradled them all the way.

Hospital Corners

1. SCAN

Together we explore my inner landscape on the screen.
He plots a course and charts me frame by frame.
See, here's your pancreas, your spleen, he chats,
and over here, this, the outline of your liver.

I watch my abdomen appear in monochrome.
Ghost-shapes float haloed, flickering like neon-signs.
I expect Apollo to land, a space-suited man step out,
glide strangely slowly across my contours with a flag.

The radiologist has moved his cursor, clicked.
The image on the monitor splits in two.
One half zooms in, zooms in again
to where circles bright as Saturn's rings

cast hard-edged shadows stretching inbetween.
Mare Frigoris, Mare Nubrium, Sea of Cold,
Sea of Clouds. *Lacus Aestruum, Oceanus Procellarum,*
Seething Lake and Ocean of Storms.

I kneel behind a crater full of stars
as data ricochets across the void. The spaceman
plants his flag in the spot marked X, leaves moonboot tracks
like 'cut-here' lines along my ovarian tract.

That night I'm in the orchard among the apple trees.
The hens have shaken out their duvets in the roots.
I slide my hand under a warmth of breast, find
a perfect egg to hold against the black. Obliterate the moon.

2. WARD MOUTH

The Ward Mouth knows everybody's business.
The Ward Mouth knows all the nurses' names
and all the nurses' boyfriends' names.
The Ward Mouth knows to the minute
when everything should happen –
Breakfast, Coffee, Lunch, Tea Break, Dinner, Night Drink.
It said so on the form.
The Ward Mouth knows *all the little tricks*
like *how the windows open* and *how to change the angle of the bed*.
The Ward Mouth knows what all the shifts are called
and that they are all *eight hours long*
except for Nights which are *two hours forty minutes longer*.
The Ward Mouth has been on
or knows somebody else who has been on
or knows somebody else who knows somebody else
who has been on every medication in the Drug Book.
She tells the Junior Houseman what he ought to do
and then tells everyone else
she *had to tell the Junior Houseman what to do*.
She can't understand what the Overseas Doctors say.
She announces this to everyone
except the Overseas Doctors.

The Ward Mouth is in the bed next to mine.
She keeps tugging my curtain back,
says it stops her seeing *one end corner of the ward*.
The Ward Mouth can't understand my need for privacy.
She thinks I'm aloof, calls me *Lady Jane* almost behind my back.
The Ward Mouth has been in here many times before.
There is not much left of her except her mouth
and, just occasionally, her fearful silence.

3. PRE-OP CHECK

I have taken my heart from the bin.
They had crumpled it up.
It had not read well.
At first, its pattern was firm,
beating the bounds of its landscape,
a heart going places,
a trustworthy heart.
Then it stumbled,
drowning its mapwork in ink.

Now the junior doctors are huddled.
They unmesh me from red and blue wires
and are blowing dust
from stethoscopes slung round their necks.
Thick books lie open
at pictures of hearts,
sections of hearts, closer close-ups.
They are speaking of murmurs and holes.
Of hooking me up again.

Which they do. I am slithery with gel.
They crowd round the printer,
tear off a length of my heart,
turn their backs, speak in whispers,
point with pens at black peaks and troughs.
My heart fills the room, riding a paper snake.
It coils on the floor, across trolleys and sinks,
loops round the blu-tacked notice above my head,
ECG out of order. Try Room 11 instead.

4. ON TOMORROW'S LIST

Apart from my measuring old moods,
the fruitbowl on the locker top
draws me in. Minute by slow minute
its shadows shift and lengthen.
The banana's liver-spots darken, expand.
Apple-pips grow loud and restless,
rattle in their cradles. Grapes
collapse in on themselves,
wear collars of mould
which have appeared greyly
as if from nowhere. Suddenly. Sooner.

This smallness, this microscopic smallness
is my act of daily living here.

I could travel out
to daily scenes I have mostly ignored.
Too familiar perhaps.
Their currency has been sand
trickling through my fingers
on a wide, endless beach.
I could hear children play, a kettle boil,
a log being split
ready for the crackle of the night.

But today, to be safest here,
these things must be left
to sweeten in silence far away.

5. OPENING DAY

Six a.m. It arrives in wan light
bears gifts in its arms.

As they draw the curtains around my bed
I unwrap each one slowly.

This, in tissue the colour of kings,
is an engraved lidded box.
It contains the fragrance of every flower
and refills as I spill some over my sheets.

The nurses come with my loose theatre-robe.
They check my pulse, tape grandmother's ring.

Here, tight in gold paper, a cut-crystal goblet
filled to the brim with
the slow ruby taste of wine.
Circling its rim, the calm conversation of friends.

I sit, propped by pillows,
and wait.

One left to open,
the shape of a long-necked jar.
It glugs when I tip it,
pours out the sounds of a sinewy sea.

Trolley wheels come close and closer.
I can hear a blackbird
fountain its notes
from a tree
far *-10*
beyond - *9*
the window – *8*
- 7

6. THEATRE

7. SISTERHOOD

We are a six-beaded rosary
bound together
for the duration of our stay.
We whisper to each other in corridors,
across our narrow beds.
   Tantum ergo sacramentum…

Sometimes we process in silence
trundling our drip stands at our sides.
We return to our stations
refreshed and cleansed by communal water,
wafers of pale communal soap.
   Pleneremur cernui…

We wake at the same hour, robed in white,
our badge of order
borne across our hearts.
We genuflect during ward rounds
wearing the same tight hose.
It matches our white knuckles
finger-counting, finger-counting
beneath the sheets
as days and nights
turn restless in their sleep.
   Et antiquum documentum…

I dreamt last night
I heard a compline bell.
An angel flew into the ward
flooding it with brilliant light
and golden benediction,
so that in the morning
each Sister of Mercy
would be blessed with a smile,
would remember our given names
as they ministered to us
in feather-white aprons.
   Novo cedat ritui…

8. OFF THE LIST

This afternoon, Ward 46 will not exist
except beneath these dressing strips,
where my wounds are trying hard to drowse
perfumed by your locker top flowers.

It's a sort of arranged marriage
those wounds and me. Stubborn too, I know
they won't let go, however hard I try
to hide or shake them free.

And I'm scared as hell I'll do the same to you
from the moment you collect me
with your wide bouquet of smiles.
At home, a cushioned chair, set just so.

No-one prepared me for this, to be discharged,
off the list, but followed by these
red-gummed beasts who, even while I sleep,
will be prowling round my head and feet.

Perhaps in time they'll choose some fresher meat
and I will reach across to guide your patient kiss,
to let your silky hands, your tongue,
glide newly down to our deep silences.

9. HOUSE MARTINS

    Scarcely a minute
I do not think of them, those loop-
the-loop pilots in gunmetal and the purest of white,
ranked tight on the telephone wires,
not even room for a single *chichirrp* between them.

    A latecomer adds his tiny weight
to the end of the row, twitter-rippling the line
with a Mexican wave of sound until every wing
is resettled, each feather lies calmed.
Perhaps the hum of conversation backwards
and forwards beneath their feet is warming.

    I passed below them yesterday
as I pulled out from the milking yard
and nudged my way through tail-flicking Friesians
on their nonchalant amble back to the field.
They hardly noticed my car,
nor my house martins festooned
in long scalloped curves
despite the Northerly wind,
the strengthening wind,
the wind they had their backs to.

    This morning, no acrobatics
over the barn, no skimming the tops of trees,
and I knew I would never see them again,
not a single one, until next year's warmth
dizzies the meadows and river banks with
fidgety flies, exposes mud to wattle and daub
the winter gaps in their half-bowl English homes.

    I imagine them now
flocking out just ahead of the frost,
crossing the Cornish coast then drawn on and into
the sun's raw warmth as it overslopes the equator.

    In a week, I will email or ring
all of Gibraltar, North Africa, Southern Spain

and ask them to look out and up
through their sky-blue windows.
Then call me back.

Hedge

Summon the things I loved first,
those small, little things that make past;
a field drowned in birdsong and dew,
a part open map,
wet air on the ruby hawthorn,
forked earth agog at clean blue,
a bonfire's whispers and musings,
its cackles and gasps, its heart,
and on a morning containing all these
is when I came across you

hedge-laying, bent to your task
with bill hook and long-handled mell,
cleaving it through at the base,
and exposing sweetness,
taking and weaving its wildness uphill.

I watched as you leaned uphill with it,
the swan-wing spread of your back
beating towards a moon crescent.
Your neck. Exposing its sweetness.
I am close to myself, and you.
Goldfinch and wren, skylark
and sparrow perch on our every finger.
Until. Even God became true
in the gloss of that grass.

So, here's the list:
toofasttooslowtooroughtoosoft
tootakemetooI'menteringyou
toomuchonewaytooturnabout
toomanyclothesontoosoonoff

andyourtrunksweredisappointing
andyoustillhadbothsocksonand
you'dnohairtospeakofinyourarmpits
andwhattherewaswasgingeryukand
Ithinkyoualwayshadoneeyeonyourvan
andonthebonfireoverthereandwhyso
quietIlikeitwhenamancancalldowntheskies
eveninhotelroomsandanywaydidyoucome
becauseifyoudiditwaspatheticand
afterwardsyoucalledmebyhername

Seeds

Down, deep into the quiet earth
they stretch and spread their roots,
driven by a common thirst
and the slake of that is deafening –
so loud, shoots rocket to the surface
with pale fingers in their ears
until, escaped and calm,
they unfurl and wave green flags –

Look, we're here…

Leaves

A bright green truck draws up at the five-bar.
Along its side is painted *'Tree SirJohns'*,
the letters brushed with texture to look like bark.

On each end of the T's crosspiece,
as well as perky leaves, is a cheerful owl who
faces a cheerful squirrel, both outlined in gold.

Then it's all hard hats and chainsaws
and, with just one break for cigarettes and bait,
the last tree round these parts is toppled.

Now its wound weeps on an open plate.
There's been a mistake, say the Council when I ring,
it shouldn't have been till next week.

Then a call from a woman down the road.
She's seen long ears that hop
and are eating all her lawn. *What are they?*

I seek her fugitive word
but our dictionaries are almost empty.
Words are being lopped and shed and

I'm struggling to find the green truck's word
beginning with a 'T' the owl and squirrel knew
when they were present tense.

If it perches in my head, before it leaves
I'll cut it in the gatepost and fence,
my door and family table,

then carve the outline of a heart around it.
Quick, while I've got it.
It's T-R-E-E. Tree. Was that it?

Learning About Bats

What is a mammal?
How can you tell which is the long-eared bat?
We learnt much that night
walking between the Douglas Firs
and round by the ponds where we halted.
Our warden waved life-size celluloid cut-outs,
the sky not yet quite the right shade of grey.

Their fingers are long and joined by twin membranes.
Only the thumb ends in a claw.
You slipped your hand inside my zip-up,
smoothly circled a nipple while
the expert explained where pipistrelles live,
how they hunt nocturnal insects like moths.
You'd set a jittery moth in my cave.

They moisten their claws with their lips and tongue
to oil their elastic wings. Once punctured, they'll die.
It's much darker now.
A huge red moon rolls from the horizon
chased by Mars. The party in front moves on,
follows the sloping path through more trees
where a man high on a ladder opens a box.

Bats' flight paths are straight, except in pursuit of food.
They capture winged insects the rate of two every second.
Then they come, skittering out of the sky,
giddy, zig-zagging between branches and stars,
between the shrieks of our group. Torches
try to hitch on their chase and can't.
Needles twitch in vectors, echolocators chirp.

Bats mate once a year by the full Autumn moon
although often the egg stays unfertilised until Spring.
You seem surprised when I unpick
the seam of your fur with my teeth, climb
through your rafters on wrists and hind feet,
to hang from the pulsing moon of your heart.
Taste your fingers. They're thick with my milk.

Draft

The poet Horace (65 - 8 BC) recommended a gap of nine years
between the writing and publication of a poem.

I am re-reading the poems I wrote about you
or rather the you I invented as you
and tried hard not to let you escape from.

Strange how my words abscond from the page,
rise like gondolas strung under sky blue balloons.
They peer down at upper and lower case fiction.

The air is thick with migrating 'hearts'
as they flee blank verse and internal rhyme.
Beating 'as one' they float from my un-lidded shoebox.

There! Three more, arm in arm, 'shell', 'shore' and 'tide'.
They leave foam-shaped gaps in the printed lines.
Then ' lighthouse', 'our boat'. A fugitive 'gull' spirals up.

'Spring tree' eases out in 'green bud', its roots dropping
clods in the margins. 'Mountain' follows
the 'blade of grass' prised out of 'your hands'.

'You' remain there repeated over and over,
first words, middle words, run-ons,
your fingers snatching at 'moons' slipping past them.

Whiteness dazzles abandoned ink, not 'moonlight'
or 'stars', they were the first to depart,
but something laid on the paper like snow.

And all I can see now are words beginning with Y
whose arms poke out from thickening drifts
trying to attract attention

like we did, when snow holed us up
nine winters ago and shaped a plot
from our hotly scribbled first draft.

Letters
For my brother

I

I have them all. Letters, quirky postcards,
airmail. Your handwriting decorates each page.
Only an architect could pace the words like you,
flourish them with curlicues, Ionic scrolls,
Corinthian ornament. And always black,
black ink from a fine gold nib. That exquisite,
viscous flow at the heel of your thoughts
as they poured like honey from your mind.
Now it's a seethe of black and yellow. Bees
from every skip and hive and mortar gap
have swarmed in. Their furious sound
has drowned you out and, although your
vocabulary still tumbles through my door,
it arrives in jumbled syntax. Undecodable.

II

Mealtimes, you and I played 'I Spy' with words
around the kitchen. It filled the gaps between
silences that chased condensation down the walls
or hung between damp clothes above us on the rack.
Mine were 'OXO' and 'OMO'. I remember 'Fyffes' too,
as much for its oval label in blue and white
as for all those 'f's. That blue, like a postcard sky.
Being older, you found the lexica of ingredients' lists.
HP and Branston stored words like 'caramel', 'molasses',
'ascetic vinegar' (A.V.), 'garlic extract', 'rutabaga'.
You taught me how their sound was shape, shape sound.
Sometimes, you would cheat and hide the words
keeping your hands around a tin or jar.
I learnt to trick you back by smearing syrup

across the outline of a lion hazed by dizzy bees,
then afterwards blame you, your sticky hands the proof.
Out of the strong came forth sweetness, we would duet.

III

A back flip, your son had said,
at first impressed,
then fleet to make the call
as your speech backwound
then slowed into a drawl
before funnelling into silence.

IV

From your hospital bed
you write me words that have no wings.
They cluster on the page and face the moon
then turn widdershins into the sun, drop
one by one from the bottom of the paper.
They sting between my fingers, in my palms,
as I try to rearrange them into sentences
we both might recognise, beginning with
'Remember when' and ending, as we always did,
with *'We'll speak soon'* and *'Love'*. But your tongue
is wreathed in words you cannot speak,
your head, an angry hive.
Your eyes are veiled in terror.
I want to force nozzles in your ears, your mouth, up
your nostrils, up your arse, even in your mute snake eye,
then work the bellows to smoke each crazed word out,
staggering and penitent. To start anew.

V

My nephew e-mails me to say you can make a cup of tea
so you're coming home. And the goldfish died. And
did I watch the final of some game show in a house?

VI

Visiting now
I have to hold the clock hands
while I skirt the outside of the church,
read its stone library of hand-carved fiction.
You'd be pointing out a Norman arch,
gargoyles the spit of family members.
And honest masonry, simple zig-zags,
a bee-bole wall hidden beneath the ivy.

But you wouldn't have seen the newish mound
shaped like a lion that I see, nor its halo of bees.
You'll not know how a sculpt of honeycomb
could taste this sharp, could taste this sweet.

Late Road Home

Nothing can erase that pale owl
moored on the metal,
the way he turned his bonneted head
to challenge my headlights.
Beak, talons, pole star bright.
A blood-red moon in his full crop.
Then, like the sure hauling of sails
for a long outward passage,
he hauled his quiet featheriness
up and into the encircling night.
Wingbeats as slow, as silent,
as this road home,
away from you.

Charcoal Burner

Each sawn length of English sycamore and beech,
elm and birch, glockenspiels across the forest floor.
Sweaty work, this thinning out
to paint in light and air for trees to breathe.
His chainsaw rivals all the crows. Woodchips fly up
then snowstorm neat-stacked blocks and billets.
A long-handled axe. He swings it down,
clefts through in one swift blow
exposing a creamy glimpse of sudden sap.
We feel the burnheat of each other's blush
and know to say nothing.

I watch him line the steel kiln;
a brashwood nest filled with quarter logs.
He gets down low with a long, straight branch
flamed in rags and petrol, then guides it in
as sweet and true as birdsong. Dryads
scurry off and hide while he drags the coned lid on
but they soon tiptoe back as the orchestra inside
tunes to a soft percussion.
When grey smoke billows gold then white,
he chimneys it and four feather plumes rise to meet
the drum-roll of woodpeckers, the woody flute of owls.

Come back tomorrow when it's cooled, he says.
The forest and I walk back through city streets.
I'm thinking of the charcoal burner in his shower,
whether he absorbs the day or washes it away.
My nose and ears prick and sharpen.
My skin thickens to a pelt that glows russet gold
beneath these sodium lights and I'm padding back
to where I saw his truck turn down a track
leading to a clearing. There, perhaps,
he'll see my pacing milk blue breast from his window.
I'll smell the kiln and hear trees grow while I wait.

Unicorn
Some things you have to believe to see

They say the first unicorn was born
in the wide arms of the Wolds.
That's why so many of their slopes are white,
where in delight it must have rolled on its back
shaking golden, cloven hooves at fluffy sky.
Shakespeare, Rilke, Lewis Carroll,
they all went there to pursue the possibility of its being.
They searched through silver woods, green lanes,
steep-sided vales, but it remained elusive
except to their industrious pens.
Somewhere, between Fimber and Thwing
or Langtoft and Huggate, Givendale and Rowley,
it was watching them. Unicorns are mild. Serene.
They have wise beards and thickly-tasselled tails
and one enchanting spiral horn
as sharp at its tip as Filey flint.
It's not true that they fight alongside lions
to uphold the honour of the Queen.
Unicorns have travelled the world, some with wings,
but they've found unpeopled barley hills
are where they want to be. If you see one,
put all your mirrors away. *Sh!*
I've seen them dipping moonlit horns in dewponds
while not being there.

Tables

I loved to be the one to open a new chalk box,
extract a pristine, silky length, a magic-stick
full of perfect numbers. I would listen to
the tap and tinkle as they were written up,
watch dust sprinkle down like fairy snow.
Sonnet-shaped, times tables filled the board.
They would hang there in white knitting,
symbol, digit interlocked row on row.

Short lines, progression and repeated images.
I suppose they had the elements of poetry.
Their music was hymnal. By five past nine
the whole school would be a-chant,
crescendos seeping under classroom doors,
long rulers pointing to the line we should be on.
Like a good kitchen table, they've served me well,
sturdy and four-square. Hidden under ours

I'd hear the clank of scale pan, thud of dough,
the gloog of beating eggs in pottery bowls.
These were my measurements of how the world
made clock hands move, how light changed sounds,
how life would always taste of new-baked bread. But
how tables can tilt and turn, tip embroidered cloths,
place-settings, monogrammed teacups, salt cellars,
napkinsfamilysilverchinamilkjugs, eggs, with them.

And how blessed I am to witness some come crashing.
I'm left with remnants of a tide table, a worn chart,
but I'll be needing neither one of them. I'll refer
to the skylark climbing her blue trill, the way-points
of silver birch and rowan, the bouquet of breakers,
their periodic gifts strewn across the sand. I thirst
for insolvable mysteries, unreachable horizons,
distances expanding to infinities. Incalculable things.

Clear Night

The night gentles and is clear
for our long outward passage.
The sky, entertaining as a pinball machine,
shoots two stars above our mast.

Yes, I would have furled you close then too.
It is something about
how we have known endings before,
how promises begin this beautiful.

Deep-keeled, we head out
past other lit silhouettes
crossing the *Separation Zone*
to slip silent along their lanes.

Beyond *Hurd Deep* you sleep below, I helm.
I am not far from myself,
nor you,
and not another masthead light in sight.

About The Author

Pat Borthwick was born in Lincoln with much of her upbringing spent on the canals and inland waterways of Britain. She now lives on a farm close to the North York Moors. Her work reflects her interest in astronomy as well as the way that terrestrial landscape and man have shaped each other. She excavates, illuminates and records language that might otherwise remain hidden or lost. Sound, sense and shape are integral elements in all her finely crafted work.

Pat Borthwick is the recipient of several Yorkshire Arts and Arts Council Awards and was awarded a Hawthornden Fellowship in 2003. She has published one previous full-length collection of poetry (Littlewood Arc) and four pamphlet collections (Pharos Press). She has published three further books resulting from her writing within rural communities.

She has been Writer in Residence for a canal, a coalmine, a cabbage and a chalk cliff as well as working in prisons and hospitals, libraries and schools. She is a founder member and former Chair of NAWE (The National Association of Writers in Education) and is currently a part-time tutor in Creative Writing for the University of Leeds and the Open College of the Arts.

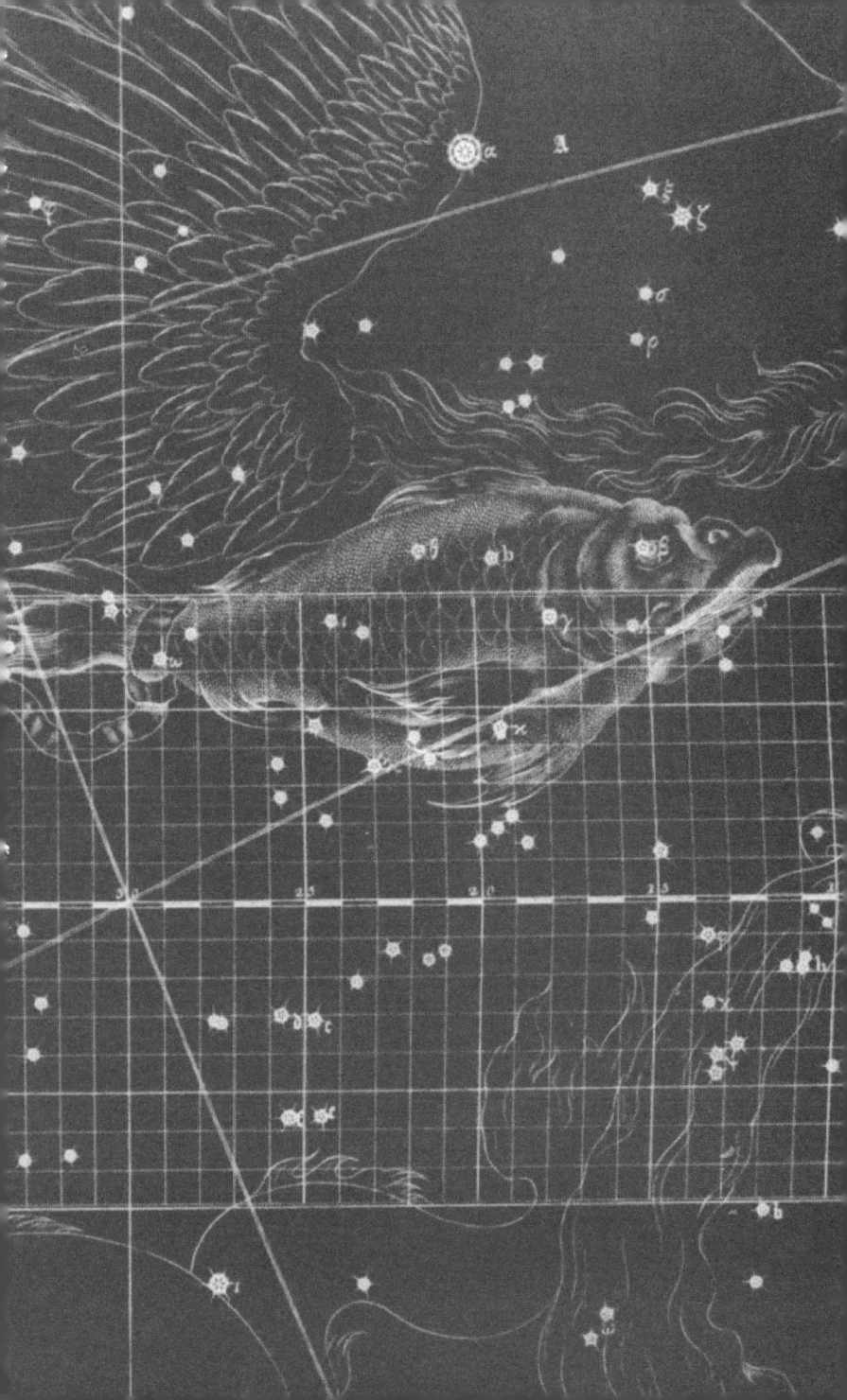